ROCKS, MINERALS, AND RESOURCES

Coal

Ron Edwards and Adrianna Edwards

Crabtree Publishing Company

www.crabtreebooks.com

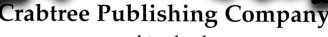

Crabtree Publishing Company

www.crabtreebooks.com

PMB 16A, 350 Fifth Avenue,
Suite 3308,
New York, NY 10118

612 Welland Avenue,
St. Catharines,
Ontario, Canada
L2M 5V6

73 Lime Walk,
Headington,
Oxford 0X3 7AD
United Kingdom

Coordinating editor: Ellen Rodger

Production coordinator: Rosie Gowsell

Designers: Brad Colotelo, Rosie Gowsell

Proofreader and Indexer: Wendy Scavuzzo

Production assistant: Samara Parent

Scanning technician: Arlene Arch-Wilson

Art director: Rob MacGregor

Photo research: Allison Napier

Prepress and printing: Worzalla Publishing Company

Consultants: Dr. Richard Cheel, Earth Sciences Department, Brock University

Project development: Focus Strategic Communication Inc.: Ron Edwards and Jenna Dunlop

Photographs: Paul Almasy/CORBIS/MAGMA: p. 31 (bottom); Bettmann/CORBIS/MAGMA: p. 13 (top), p. 13 (bottom), p. 22 (top), p. 22 (bottom), p. 23; Jonathan Blair/CORBIS/MAGMA: p. 19 (bottom); MARTIN BOND/SCIENCE PHOTO LIBRARY: p. 24 (bottom); Andy Butler; Eye Ubiquitous/CORBIS/MAGMA: p. 7; Nancy Durrell-McKenna: p. 21; Ed Eckstein/CORBIS/MAGMA: cover; Jeff Greenberg/Maxximages.com: p. 16; Chinch Gryniewicz; Ecoscene/CORBIS/MAGMA: p. 29 (right); Jan Halaska/ Maxximages.com: p. 25; Michael Heller/911 Pictures: title page; Hulton Archive Laister: p. 18; Hulton-Deutsch Collection/CORBIS/MAGMA: p. 12; Wolfgang Kaehler/CORBIS/MAGMA: p. 31 (top); Chuck Keefer/Getty Images: p. 24 (top); Keystone/Maxximages.com: p. 9 (right); larry Lee Photography/CORBIS/MAGMA: background image; Andrew J. Martinez/Photo Researchers, Inc.: p. 8; Northwind Picture Archives: p. 11; Art Directors/Mike Peters: p. 19 (top); Joel W. Rogers/CORBIS/MAGMA: p. 27 (bottom); Charles E. Rotkin/CORBIS/MAGMA: p. 29 (left); Karlene V. Schwartz: p. 9 (left); Chris Stowers: p. 10; Dieter Telemans: p. 15, p. 27 (top);

Michael S. Yamashita/CORBIS/MAGMA: p. 20. All other images from stock photo CD

Illustrations: Robert MacGregor: p. 6, p. 26; Dan Pressman: p. 14, p. 17 (all), p. 28; Margaret Amy Reiach: title page, pp. 4-5

Map: Jim Chernishenko; p. 21

Cover: A coal miner pushes a cartload of coal on tracks in a West Virginia railyard.

Title page: Coal miners often emerge from mines covered in black coal dust.

38888000067318

Published by
Crabtree Publishing Company

Copyright © **2004**

Cataloging-in-Publication Data

Edwards, Ron, 1947-
  Coal / Ron Edwards & Adrianna Edwards.
    p. cm. -- (Rocks, minerals, and resources)
  Includes index.
    ISBN 0-7787-1410-1 (rlb) -- ISBN 0-7787-1442-X (pbk.)
  1. Coal--Juvenile literature. I. Edwards, Adrianna, 1954- II. Title. III. Series.
  TN801.E39 2004
  553.2'4--dc22
                                      2004000805
                                      LC

Contents

What is coal?

The alarm sounded, signaling trouble in the mine. Those who heard it feared for their friends and loved ones working underground. There was a noise like thunder and a ground-shaking rumble. The sound of an explosion in the mine always struck terror in the hearts of mining families.

Mining Coal

Coal mining is much safer today than in past centuries but it is still a risky undertaking performed under difficult conditions. Coal provides a lot of the world's energy and has long been an important part of our lives. Coal is a **natural resource** and **fossil fuel** used to generate electricity for heating, lighting, and manufacturing.

How coal was forme

About 300 million years ago, most of the Earth was covered with lush green plants that grew in swamps. This era of time when coal formed is called the Carboniferous Period. It is also called the Coal Age.

Coal Formation

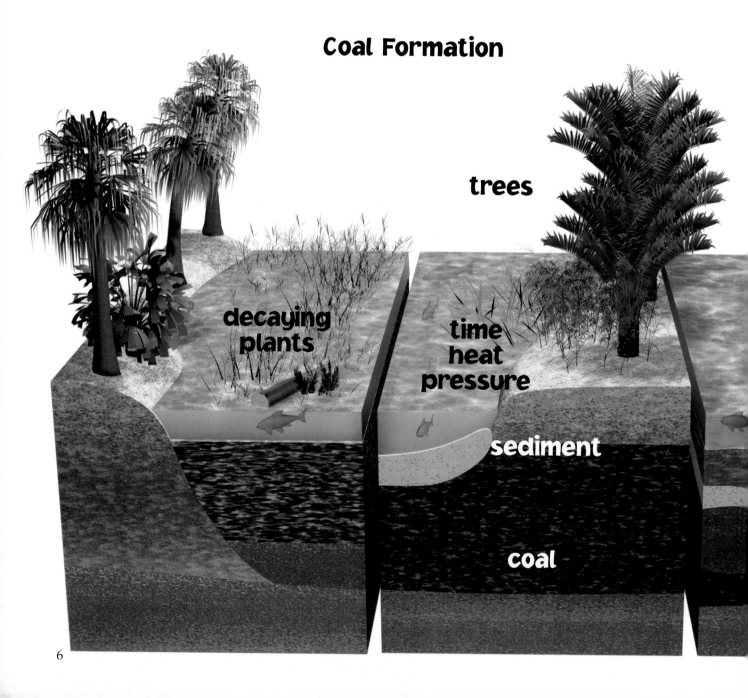

trees

decaying plants

time
heat
pressure

sediment

coal

From trees to coal

During the Carboniferous Period, the Earth was covered with lush forests, lakes, and oceans full of life. When trees and plants died and fell into the water, they began to decay, or break down. The carbon and the other elements in the plants and other living things could not drain out.

Over time, mud and sand **sediment** covered the rotting plant and animal matter. Eventually, many layers of sediment built up, increasing the pressure, or weight from above, on the decaying plant and animal matter. The decayed plants and animals dried and hardened to form carbon-rich coal.

What is coal?

Coal is a natural resource made of tiny particles called atoms. Atoms are too small to be seen by the human eye. There are many different types of atoms, but they are all called elements. Coal is made up of the elements carbon, **hydrogen**, and **oxygen**. Carbon is the most common element in living things.

Coal is an organic rock, meaning it was created from the decayed remains of living things.

Types of coal

There are many different types of coal. Some coal burns better than others and some is harder and darker. Each type of coal is used for a different purpose.

There are four main types of coal. The types, or ranks are based on how much water the coal contains. Harder coal has less water and is a better fuel because it burns more efficiently.

No carbon copies

Each type of coal contains a different amount of carbon, **nitrogen**, oxygen, and **sulphur**. Carbon is the part of coal that burns well and gives off heat. The more carbon there is in the coal, the better it will burn. The amount of carbon in coal is known as the carbon content.

Lignite

Lignite is often called brown coal. It is crumbly and very soft because it contains a lot of water. When lignite formed, it was not buried as deep or **compressed** as hard, so it has a higher water content. It is located close to the Earth's surface and is easily mined.

Lignite does not burn very well and is not the best coal to use for fuel.

Sub-bituminous coal

Sub-bituminous coal is harder than lignite, but is still crumbly. It is dark brown or black and is used as a fuel in industry.

Bituminous coal

Bituminous coal is a hard, dark coal. In the past, it was used to heat homes. Bituminous coal is burned for energy in industries, such as steel making, and in generating electricity. This type of coal is most commonly used because it burns well and produces a lot of heat. Bituminous coal is not buried very deep underground, which means it is not very expensive to mine. There is a lot of bitumous coal buried within the Earth, which means supplies are plentiful.

Anthracite

Anthracite is called black coal, hard coal, or peacock coal because it is very hard, black, and shiny. It is found deep under the ground. Anthracite is considered the best type of coal because it burns well and at a high temperature. It is used in industry and is the most rare and expensive type of coal to mine.

Peat

Peat is a type of fuel that is dug out of the ground, dried, and burned. In some countries, peat is still used for cooking and for heating houses. In Finland, Ireland, and Russia, peat is used to produce electricity.

Like coal, peat forms in **bogs**. If peat were left buried for thousands more years, it would turn into coal. When peat is dug up, it looks like **decayed** wood. It is very wet, but can be burned when dried out.

For centuries, peat has been burned for fuel in Finland.

Coal in history

Coal has been important to many peoples and cultures throughout history. Anthropologists, or scientists who study human cultures, have discovered that coal was used to make cooking fires more than 6,000 years ago.

The people of the Roman Empire, which lasted from about 27 B.C. to 410 A.D., used coal for heating, cooking, and working with metal. The use of coal was spread from England to Egypt as the Romans expanded their **empire**. By the Middle Ages, a period of time from 500 A.D. to 1500 A.D., coal was being mined in western Europe. Beginning in the 1200s, people in China used coal fires to heat, melt, and reshape copper and **cast iron**. Coal was also used in North America in the 1400s when the Hopis, native peoples of the southwestern United States, dug coal and used it to fire, or bake and harden, their pottery.

A family collects coal for heating and cooking near a coal mine in China. Coal fires have been used in China since the 1200s.

Coal mines supplied factories with fuel during the Industrial Revolution. By the late 1700s to early 1800s, factories produced clothing and steel for the growing markets.

Industrial Revolution

In the late 1700s to early 1800s, people in western Europe began to use machines to make products that people used to make by hand. This period of time is called the Industrial Revolution because it changed the way people worked and lived.

Unlike other revolutions, the Industrial Revolution was not a fight against a government or a political system. It was a brutal and quick change from farming and small home workshops, to large scale industry. Before factories were created, people usually worked at home with family members.

In the 1700s in most of the world, wood was still the main source of fuel for cooking and heating fires. Things changed when new metals such as steel, began to be used in massive quantities in big factories. Steel was stronger and lighter than iron and other metals. It allowed bigger and better machines to be built in these factories. Coal, which burned hotter than wood, became the fuel used in factories.

Age of manufacturing

Machines in factories did the work faster than humans did by themselves or in small craft workshops. Factory owners paid workers to run the machines. Factory work moved people away from farms and country villages to the cities. Coal was the fuel used to build and run the factory machines.

The steam engine

In the mid-1700s, a strange new machine changed the way people lived. In 1765, Scottish inventor James Watt redesigned the steam engine to run more efficiently. Steam engines were very powerful. They allowed factories to make more goods at a faster pace.

Coal was the fuel used to power machines during the Industrial Revolution. This man is stoking, or tending, a coal-fired engine in a factory.

Coal and steam

Factories used steam to make engines run. The steam came from heating water, just as steam comes from boiling water in a pot. The first steam engines burned wood, and then coal was used because it made fires burn hotter and longer. Coal also took up less space than wood, so it was easier to store.

Until the steam engine, coal had only been mined from just under the surface of the Earth. The steam engine made it possible to dig deeper for coal, and mining began on a large scale. Before the steam engine, deep mines would flood and there was no way to get the water out. The steam engine was used to pump water out.

Steam trains used coal as fuel. By the 1940s, most steam trains were replaced by diesel.

Coal miners ride an elevator to work deep beneath the Earth.

Finding coal

Finding coal under the Earth's surface is a science. Geologists are scientists who study the physical geography of the Earth and how it was formed. They use their knowledge of the Earth's structure to find out where coal is buried.

Geologists know coal is found in areas that were covered by swamps millions of years ago. Over time, the swamps were covered with plant and animal matter that compressed and became **sedimentary rock**. Coal is formed inside the rock in layers called seams. Sedimentary rock formations are studied and mapped by geologists. When they locate what they believe is a seam of coal in sedimentary rock, they test by drilling into the ground and taking samples.

Core drills

For an exact picture of what is in the rock below the surface, special drills called core drills are used. Core drills are hollow tubes with diamond tips. Diamond-tipped drills are very hard and can easily slice through the rock underground. Drillers bring a solid round **core sample** to the surface. These cores show if there are any coal seams, where they are, and how big they are.

A coal deposit that is close to the surface is much easier to find. Machines, such as bulldozers, strip away the soil and uncover the coal. The coal is then collected by machines, or by hand.

The rock cycle: rock is formed in a cyclical process.

Other methods of finding coal

Modern science makes looking for coal easier. Today, many different methods, such as aerial photographs, are used to find coal. Aerial photographs are taken by planes flying above land where geologists believe coal is located. Geologists examine the images and the topography, or physical features, of the land for clues that lead to coal.

There are other ways to look under the ground to find coal. Geologists also use **magnetic pulses** and radar waves to locate seams. If the radar waves hit hard objects underground, such as rock, they bounce back. The bounced, or reflected, waves show the structure of the rock underground in an electronic image. Hard rock and coal reflect different images that geologists then "read" to determine the size and location of the coal deposit.

(above) Workers labor in an open-pit coal mine in Fushun, China. The mine, which was opened in 1914, is the largest in China. It is no longer profitable and miners are losing their jobs.

15

Coal mining

Coal is found both close to the surface of the Earth and buried deep underground. There are two main methods of mining coal. The way coal is mined depends on where it is located and how deeply it is buried.

Surface mining or strip mining

Surface mining is one way coal is mined. Surface mining is also called open-pit mining and strip mining because the coal is located close to the surface of the land and is "stripped" from the Earth. Strip mining leaves the land scarred, gashed, and without trees and ground cover. It is less expensive to surface mine, or strip mine, for coal.

Surface, or strip, mines are used when the coal is not buried too deeply.

Underground mining

When coal is buried deep underground, mines are dug to reach it. There are three types of underground mines. Shaft mines use a vertical shaft, or tunnel, to reach the coal seam. Miners descend the shaft and dig the coal out using machinery and hand tools.

Slope mines also have shafts to get to the coal, but they are built on an angle. Slope mines are built when it is too hard or too dangerous to build a shaft straight down.

Drift mines are used when the coal is found in the side of a mountain. They have horizontal tunnels, known as drifts, instead of vertical shafts.

Shaft mine

Drift mine

Slope mine

Dangers in coal mines

In the early days of mining, coal mines were dangerous places to work. Even today, cave-ins, explosions, and poison gases are great dangers to miners.

When coal is removed from mines, it leaves large hollowed-out pockets underground. In early mines, wooden beams called props held up the walls and the ceiling. Sometimes, the enormous weight of the earth above became too heavy and the walls and ceiling collapsed. Today, coal miners use steel shafts to support the roof. Sometimes, they leave large pillars of coal in the rock, which helps to support the shafts and tunnels and prevent cave-ins.

Other dangers

Digging sometimes releases poison gases trapped in the rock. The gases killed miners who breathed them. A fresh-air shaft was dug beside the mine shaft to get clean air into the mine. By the 1900s, fans were added to the shafts and tunnels to keep fresh air circulating through the mine.

Coal dust in mines is explosive and dangerous to breathe in. The dust sometimes sparked fires that set off chain-reaction explosions caused by the gases in the mine. Today, explosions and fires are still a danger for coal miners

Bird bait

In the early 1800s, miners took caged canaries down into coal mines. The birds were used to test for deadly mine gases. The tiny birds died after breathing small amounts of the gases. This alerted miners to the presence of gases they could not smell or see. The miners were then able to leave the mines before they too died from the gases.

Sorting and cleaning coal

After coal is removed from the rock, it is separated and sorted according to size. Bigger pieces are crushed down to a smaller size. The coal is then sifted through a filter screen. The screens divide coal into coarse, medium, or fine sizes.

Coal is also cleaned of **impurities**, such as sulphur. Impurities make the coal dirty, and poisonous to burn. Cleaning the coal reduces the pollution. The impurities weigh more than the coal, so when the coal is washed in water, the impurities sink to the bottom. The coal is then dried.

Coal is sorted by size, using a filter screen.

Shipping coal

Once coal has been mined, sorted, and cleaned, it is ready to be **processed**. Processing plants are usually located away from the mine. After processing, the coal is transported to where it will be used. Most coal is used in electrical plants or steel mills.

In North America, two thirds of the coal from mines and processing plants is moved by railroad.

Coal deposits

Coal is found in almost every part of the world. The earliest known coal mine was the Fushun mine in northeastern China. It was mined over 3,000 years ago. Today, China has nearly half of the world's proven, or explored, coal deposits.

There are more than 2,000 major coal deposits located around the world. Today, China, the United States, India, and Australia are the largest producers of coal. Much of the coal that is mined is used for fuel in the country where it is mined. The United States produces 930 million tons (844 million tonnes) of coal each year, but only **exports** 43 million tons (39 million tonnes).

Many of China's coal mines are open-pit operations, where the coal is dug out of above-ground mines and collected by hand. These people are collecting coal to use at home at the mining town of Ma Lin, China.

World coal deposits

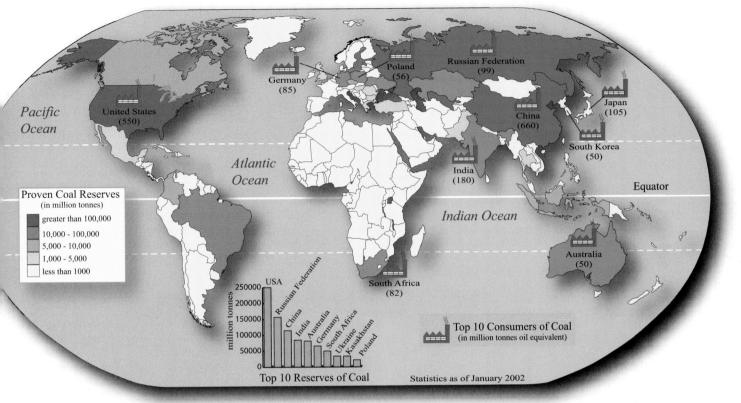

Proven Coal Reserves
(in million tonnes)

- greater than 100,000
- 10,000 - 100,000
- 5,000 - 10,000
- 1,000 - 5,000
- less than 1000

Germany (85)
United States (550)
Poland (56)
Russian Federation (99)
Japan (105)
China (660)
South Korea (50)
India (180)
South Africa (82)
Australia (50)

Pacific Ocean
Atlantic Ocean
Indian Ocean
Equator

Top 10 Reserves of Coal

Top 10 Consumers of Coal
(in million tonnes oil equivalent)

Statistics as of January 2002

A coal miner pushes a car full of coal in an underground mine in South Africa.

World Coal Production

Country	Amount of Coal Produced (million tonnes)
China	1,294
U.S.A.	945
India	312
Australia	257
South Africa	225
Russia	168
Poland	104
Indonesia	92.5
Ukraine	82
Kazakhstan	73

A miner's life

Mining is hard physical work. Miners have often had to work under terrible conditions. The air in the mines was hard to breathe, there was no light, and it was cold and wet. Sometimes, the tunnels were so small that miners could not even stand upright.

Most people worked in mines because there was no other work available. In many mining communities, all jobs depended on the mine.

Company towns

In the 1900s, many coal mines were located in remote areas, far from major cities. Coal companies built company towns where the company owned all of the houses, schools, and stores. Some mining companies even paid miners their own paper money called scrip. Scrip could be used only at the company store. The mining company's stores controlled prices and the supply of goods. Many miners did not earn very much and often could not support their families. They had to borrow from the company just to get by. As a result, miners were rarely able to get out of debt.

Coal mining was very dangerous. The chances of dying in a cave-in or an explosion were high. Often, there were no safety regulations.

Mule-drawn coal carts removed coal from the mines.

Unions

Miners fought to form unions that represented their interests as workers. The mining companies did not want the workers to unionize because it meant workers could fight together for better pay and working conditions. Unionized miners could go on strike, depriving the company of their labor. Mining companies threatened workers who joined unions and sometimes hired men to beat up union organizers.

In most parts of the world, conditions in mines have improved in the last 20 years. Governments have imposed safety **regulations** and unions have helped improve wages, health care, and **pensions** for miners. Despite this, mining is still a difficult and dangerous job.

Coal miners rally in Washington to protest government cuts to health programs for miners. Black lung and silicosis are two lung diseases caused by breathing coal dust in the mines. Many miners died young from these diseases.

Harlan County, U.S.A.

In the 1900s, Harlan County, Kentucky like many coal mining communities, was one of the poorest areas in the United States. Many people lived in company housing that did not have indoor plumbing or running water. The mines in Harlan County were the scene of many long and bitter strikes by coal miners. In 1973, a strike lasted for an entire year, because the miners had joined a union and the mining company refused to sign a contract with the miners. Their long strike and the lives of the miners who joined the union was filmed in an **Academy Award**-winning **documentary**.

Uses of coal

Coal is a reliable and affordable energy source. Before the days of central heating and gas and oil furnaces, many people used coal to heat their homes and cook their food.

In some parts of the world, such as India, China, and Africa, people still use coal for cooking and heating. In these areas, coal is cheaper and readily available. In many other areas of the world, **natural gas** and electricity have replaced coal for heating and cooking.

Coal used to be kept in special buckets called scuttles near the fireplace, where it would be used to heat a home.

Electricity

Some countries, such as the United States and Germany, rely on coal to produce more than half of their electricity. Australia and China produce over three quarters of their electricity from burning coal. Electricity-generating plants use heat from burning coal to power turbines and engines to make electricity. Burning the coal is called coal firing because the coal fires produce the energy needed to make the electricity.

Almost 40 percent of the world's electricity is made from coal. These coal stacks are located at a coal-fired electricity-generating station.

Coal in industry

Today, most commercially mined coal is used in industry to make electricity and as a fuel for manufacturing. Coal is a plentiful fuel and is easy and safe to transport and store.

The steel industry depends on coal. Steel manufacturing plants need incredibly hot fires to make steel. Steel makers have found ways of making coal burn even hotter than it normally does. To do this, coal is placed in an airtight furnace and impurities are burned off. The remaining pure coal is called coke. Pure coke burns much hotter than regular coal.

Steel plants need very hot fires to melt and shape metals. They use a material called coke, which is made from coal, to make their blast furnaces hotter.

25

Pollution from coal

In the early 1800s, England was famous for its fog. The island country is surrounded by ocean, but the fog did not just come from the wet weather. The fog also came from burning coal fires.

England's famous fogs came from the household burning of lignite. Lignite is a grade of coal that burns less cleanly than higher grades. It created a lot of smoke that mixed with the weather fogs of England to produce a dirty smog. The smog continued until lignite was replaced by better coals and, later, widespread use of electricity to heat homes and cook food.

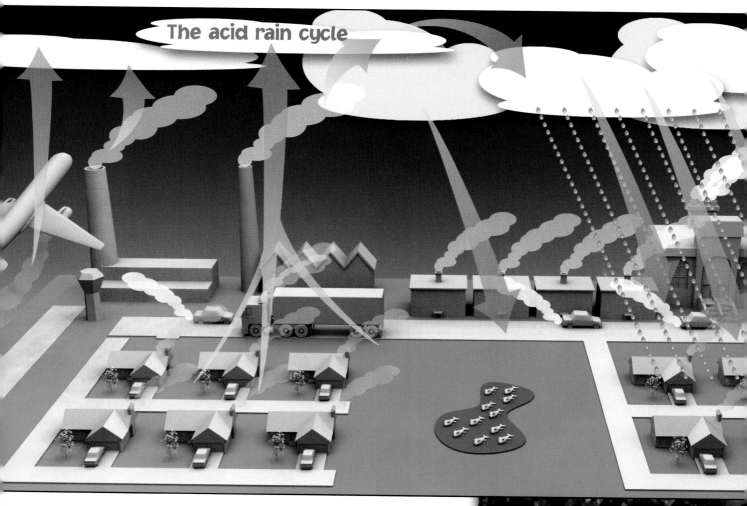

The acid rain cycle

Acid rain

Acid rain is a form of pollution created when coal is burned. When chemicals released by burning coal mix with rainwater, the water becomes poisonous. The smoke created when coal is burned comes out of tall smokestacks at steel plants and electricity-generating stations. The smoke carries chemicals and gases that are spread far away from the smokestack by air currents. The gases mix with water drops in the air and clouds and create acid rain. When the acid rain falls, it can be hundreds or even thousands of miles away from the smokestack. Acid rain looks exactly like normal rain but over time, the chemicals in the rain poison plants, fish, and animals. Lakes damaged by acid rain are called dead lakes because they no longer support fish, plant, and animal life.

Pollution from coal-fired electricity plants, and factories that use coal to make steel, is harming the environment.

Global warming

Scientists believe that burning fossil fuels, such as coal, contributes to global warming and the greenhouse effect. Global warming happens when heat from the Sun gets trapped in the Earth's atmosphere. The greenhouse effect occurs when the heat raises temperatures around the Earth.

Earth's atmosphere

The Earth is surrounded by layers of gases called the atmosphere. Heat from the Sun comes through the atmosphere and warms the Earth. Usually, this heat bounces off the Earth and back out through the atmosphere into space. When coal is burned, it produces carbon dioxide. Carbon dioxide mixes with water vapor in the air, and creates an invisible ceiling in the Earth's atmosphere. The ceiling acts like a greenhouse and keeps the sun's heat in. If the air around the Earth keeps getting warmer, scientists believe the Arctic ice caps and glaciers will melt and lead to flooding. They also believe droughts will occur more frequently as the Earth's climate changes.

Coal mining can lead to landscape pollution. After coal mines stop producing, they are often abandoned, leaving behind ugly defaced landscapes. In West Virginia, a process called mountain top mining has destroyed hundreds of acres of land near mines. The earth and debris above the mountain coal mines is removed and dumped near valleys and steams.

Earth's atmosphere has several layers. Burning coal damages the layer closest to the Earth's crust.

Cleaning coal

As the world's population grows, the demand for fossil fuels increases. More people will need these fuels to provide heat and power for their homes. Increased demand means more pollution. Scientists have been working on making coal cleaner to burn by turning it into a liquid or a gas. Some companies that use coal are also trying to make the smoke less harmful to the environment by attaching scrubbers that act like filters to their smokestacks to keep the dangerous gases from escaping into the air.

Many abandoned coal mines have been reclaimed.

Reclaimed mines

Many countries have laws that require mining companies to clean up the land they used for mining. Mining companies have to make the land look the same as it did before it was mined. This is called reclaiming the land. The mining companies turned the ugly wastelands into farmland, public parks, playgrounds, and wildlife **habitats**. The U.S. state of Illinois, reclaimed over 5,000 acres (2,023 hectares) of coal-mined land.

Alternatives to coal

The world is in no danger of running out of coal. Scientists predict coal supplies will last another 3,000 years, but coal's effect on the environment is leading many to look for other, less harmful energy sources.

Wind power

Coal and other fossil fuels, such as oil and natural gas, are non-renewable energy sources. Many scientists and governments are trying to replace them with renewable energy sources that can be used again. Wind energy is one renewable resource that is clean and cheap to use. Windmills have been used for thousands of years for grinding wheat or pumping water. Today, wind turbines are being built to generate electricity. Some scientists think that they will produce ten percent of the world's electricity by 2030.

Niagara Falls is the largest source of hydroelectric power in the world. Every minute, 35 million gallons (133 million liters) of water fall over the edge.

Water power

Water is another renewable resource. People have used the power of falling water for thousands of years. Water wheels turn when water falls on them and create energy. In the past, these water wheels were attached to pumps or millstones for grinding grain into flour.

Today, giant water wheels, or turbines, are used to produce electricity. Falling water turns the blades on turbines, which turn the generator to produce electricity in hydroelectric power stations. Large waterfalls, such as Niagara Falls, are used to produce hydroelectric power.

Geothermal power

In some countries, the Earth's heat is used to generate electricity and heat homes. Geothermal energy is energy produced from steam heated by magma, liquid rock located near the Earth's core. The hot magma rises and heats water and rock below the Earth's surface. The steam rises to Earth's surface and escapes through volcanoes, geysers, and hot springs. Some countries, such as the U.S., Iceland, New Zealand, and the Philippines, use geothermal power to create electricity. In Iceland, geothermal power is used to heat 95 percent of the homes in the country. Geothermal energy is renewable and does not pollute.

Rotorua, New Zealand, is heated by energy from the steam produced by its hot springs. This woman cooks supper in an outdoor steam pit.

Glossary

Academy Award An American film award

bogs Areas of land that are soft and water-soaked

carbon A non-metallic element formed in organic matter

cast iron A hard and brittle form of iron that is often shaped into furniture and fences

compressed Squeezed or pressed tightly together

core sample A piece of rock brought to the surface by drilling, and used by geologists

decayed Rotted

documentary A film or TV show that tells a real story about a political, social, or historical event, usually by news clips, interviews, and narration

empire A large territory or group of territories controlled by a single ruler

exports Surplus goods traded or sold to another country

fossil fuel A fuel, such as coal or gas, that formed millions of years ago from the remains of dead plants and animals

habitats The places where plants and animals naturally live

hydrogen A light gas that burns easily and is a component of water

impurities Unwanted parts

magnetic pulses Short bursts of waves that can detect metals

natural gas A fossil fuel formed from the remains of dead plants

natural resource Something found in nature that is useful to people, such as water, forests, metals, and fossil fuels

nitrogen A colorless, odorless gas

oxygen A colorless, odorless gas that humans and animals breathe

pensions Money paid to people who have retired from work

processed A series of actions in which something is made into another form

regulations Rules or laws

sediment Small pieces of matter, usually sand or stone, that are deposited by water or wind

sedimentary rock A type of rock formed from the build up and eventual compression of many layers of sediment

sulphur A yellow-colored chemical that smells like rotten eggs

Index

1 2 3 4 5 6 7 8 9 0   Printed in the USA   0 9 8 7 6 5 4 3 2 1